# I LIKE ME T.M.

Author: Blanche P. Gaston
Illustrator: Aaron Kerns

The I LIKE ME Publishing Co.
I LIKE ME, INC.
CHICAGO, ILLINOIS 60628

Library of Congress Catalogue Card Number 37-238
ISBN:
0-9608516-0-7
0-9608516-1-5
Printed in the United States of America

The I LIKE ME Publishing Co.
I LIKE ME, INC.
CHICAGO, ILLINOIS  60628

Dedicated to:
My daughter,
Gina,
and the millions of children
around the world, with the
hope of building positive
self concepts.

I like my face.
It's round like the moon.
I look in the mirror,
And pretty soon —

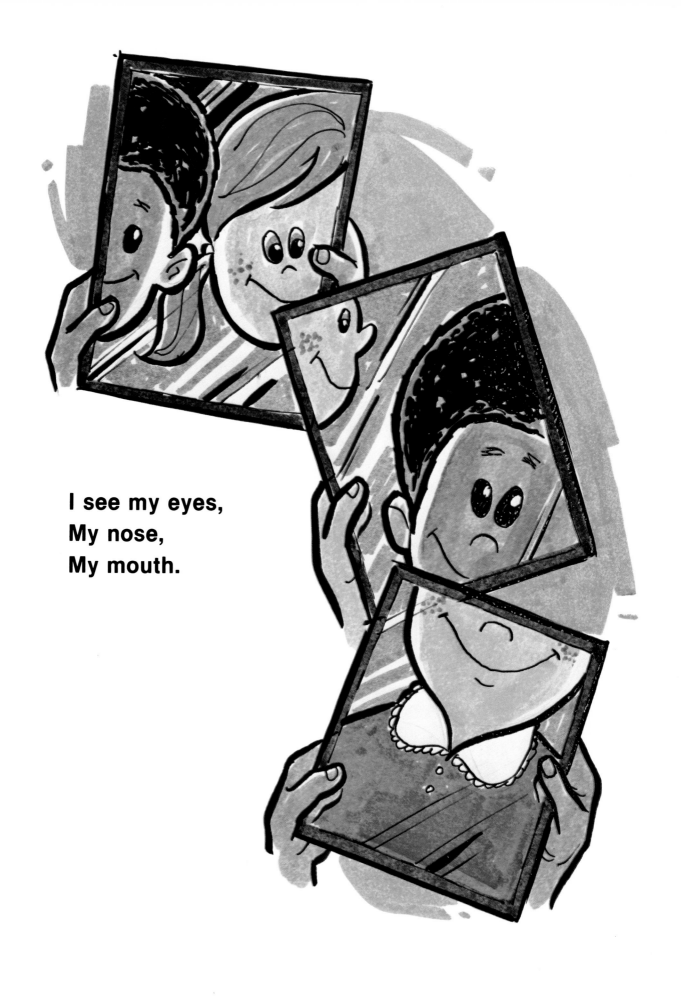

I see my eyes,
My nose,
My mouth.

My eyes glow back
To show the color.
My eyes are gray.
What color are yours?
Brown? Blue? Black? or Gray?
Whatever the color,
They'll be that way.
They are beautiful
And here to stay.

I like my nose;
It smells sweet things.
Smells beautiful flowers
After spring showers.
It allows me to breathe
The air around me.
What shape is your nose?
I wonder?

The shape of my mouth
is like a boat.
How is your mouth
shaped? I'd like to know.
I like what it eats.
I eat what it likes.
The things I think come
out of my mouth.
I'm careful about what I say.
Thank you! You're welcome!
Have a good day!

My ears hear things no one else hears.
They hear the sounds of the city
And the country near.
What sounds do you hear?
Boom! Bang! Zzzm!
Or the chatter of the animals clear?

My skin is my cover.
I like it so.
What color is your skin?
Do you know?
Is it brown? Is it white? Is it black?
Is it chocolate? Peachy? Creamy white?

I like my hands.
They tell me what to do.
Are your hands busy?
Are they a part of you?
What do you do with your hands?
Paint a picture and
build a toy house?
This is what hands are all about.
Use your hands to help you.

My arms I need
in everything I do.
Hug my Mom in
love and appreciation, too.
What things do you do?
Don't be alarmed,
If it's millions
of things you do
with your arms.

My legs take me to many places,
Shopping with Mom,
And I meet many faces.
They help me to walk
Where I want to go.
My legs, I like
And appreciate so.

I have a body.
That stands so tall.
How tall are you?
Or, even how small?
The body is useful in many ways.
It helps hold our legs,
arms and head,
So we can use them
in the proper ways.
I like my body.
It's special.

I like my muscles,
bones, and things!
They have a purpose, too.
I use them in everything I do.
They hold my skin on.
They give my body shape.
These parts of my body
are useful.

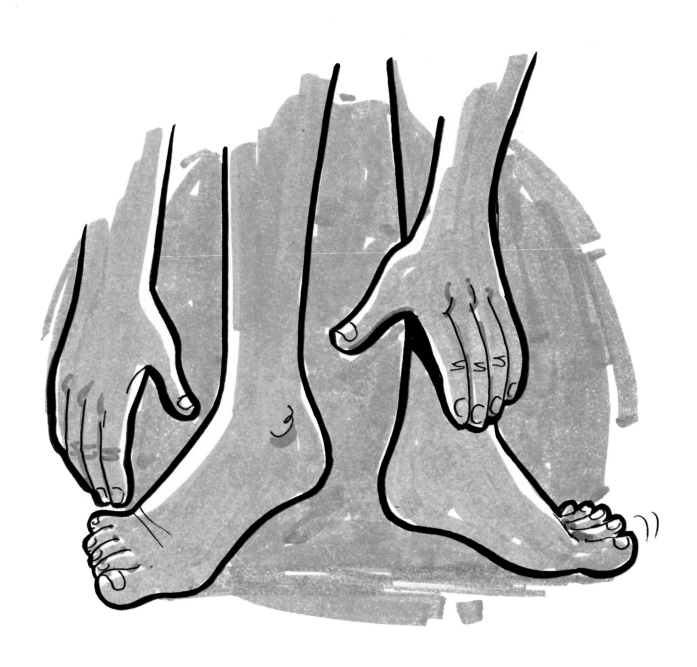

I like my fingers, feet, and toes.
They are very important
As everyone knows —

My fingers help me to feel.
They help me to find my way in the dark.
They help me to catch
The baseball in the park.

I can't do without my feet.
My feet are an important
part of me.
They hold my body
And keep me from falling.
They help me when
I start prancing.
They are graceful
When I am dancing.

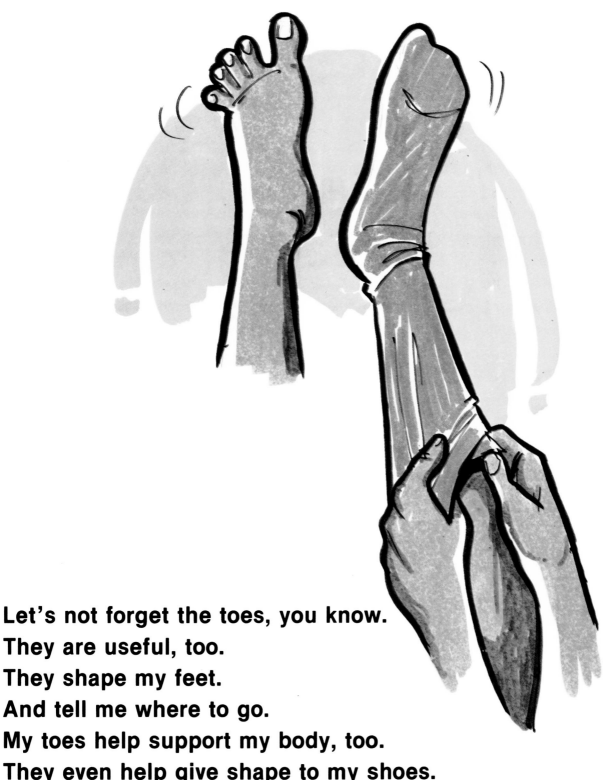

Let's not forget the toes, you know.
They are useful, too.
They shape my feet.
And tell me where to go.
My toes help support my body, too.
They even help give shape to my shoes.
I remember my toes,
Wherever I go.

Remember to keep
your mind on you.
Keep your mind on you
whatever you do.

Let's not forget others, too.
Appreciate the things they do.

I like me.
I like you, too.
I like people —
All kinds of people,
All kinds of sizes,
All kinds of shapes,
People —
With all kinds of faces.

I like me.
I like you.
Draw you!
Draw me, too!

**DRAW YOU**                    **DRAW ME**

## I LIKE ME T.M. — song

I LIKE ME.
I LIKE ME.
I LIKE ME.
I REALLY LIKE ME.
I SHARE MY LOVE.
YES, I DO.
I LIKE YOU, TOO.